Dessert Cocktails

Classic and Contemporary After-Dinner Drinks

Michelle Dompierre Southern

PORTLAND, OREGON

*To my best friend and husband, who has clinked many
a glass with me and lived to tell the tale.*

XO~M

Copyright © 2007 Michelle Dompierre Southern

Cover Design: Kevin A. Welsch
Designers: Sara E. Blum, Kaya Dzankich
Editors: Jennifer Weaver-Neist, Lindsay S. Brown

Library of Congress Cataloging-in-Publication Data

Dompierre-Southern, Michelle.
  Dessert cocktails: classic and contemporary after
dinner drinks / by Michelle Dompierre-Southern.
-- 1st American ed.
       p.   cm.
Includes index.
  ISBN 1-933112-29-8 (hardcover : alk. paper)
1. Cocktails. 2. Desserts. I. Title.
TX951.D66 2007
641.8'74--dc22

                    2006028825

Distributed by Publisher Group West
ISBN 10: 1-933112-29-8
ISBN 13: 978-1-933112-29-9

First American Edition
Printed in China
9 8 7 6 5 4 3 2 1

Table of Contents

Introduction

It's late. The sun is setting, the moon is rising. You've just enjoyed a fabulous dinner with friends—or maybe with your heart's desire. It's time for something sweet to indulge in, but cheesecake or a sundae seems too heavy and rich. What can you serve that will spark conversation, delight your guests, and signal the end of the meal? Why, a dessert cocktail, of course!

Who do we have to thank for cocktails? There are as many stories about their beginnings and definitions for the term as there are people to drink them. After-dinner cocktails were created not to quench a thirst, but for pure enjoyment and indulgence before heading off to sleep (which is why they are sometimes referred to as a "nightcap").

Liqueurs, typically being the sweetest and most seductive of the bunch, are perfect dessert drinks on their own. But they can also be used as a topping for ice cream, a marinade for fruit, or a sinful addition to brewed coffee. Drinkable desserts are also sipped, not gulped, and are more relaxing after a heavy or long supper. With designer coffees being so expensive, why spend megabucks at fancy cafés and trendy chains when you can stay in and make tastier versions yourself?

The two most common questions people ask about dessert drinks are, "What do I serve?" and "Does the drink need to match the food?" It's really quite simple. You decide by considering the guests you've invited. Non-drinkers will savor mocktails (nonalcoholic cocktails also known as "smartinins"), java junkies will enjoy delicious dessert cocktail coffees, and even dieters can enjoy indulgent drinks when you use diet or low-calorie mixers and sugarless sweeteners. Your friends will be delighted when you offer any kind of twist on "the usual."

If you aren't too sure about the guests' personalities, think about the location, time, season, and setting of your dinner. For a summer patio party, serve frozen cocktails. When viewing the sunset on the balcony, serve tropical drinks. While hanging out by the fireside after an evening of caroling, serve hot, mulled drinks or eggnog sippers. And themed parties have the easiest selection: just serve classic cocktails from the era you're celebrating or drinks that match the occasion.

For a crowd-pleasing favorite, offer dessert coffees. You can select from any high-quality, dark roast coffee or espresso available at your grocery store or coffee shop—along with a good decaf version—and provide a choice of liqueurs, sweeteners, toppings, and whipped cream. Sprinkles, chocolate shavings, and spices such as ground cinnamon are easy garnishes.

Although it's so tempting to want to drink a sweet concoction with your meal, you are saving the best for last with dessert cocktails. They allow you to enjoy an after-dinner conversation without talking with your mouth full. A served drink at the conclusion of supper also tells guests that the meal is over, allowing the party to move into another area to relax and talk. Dieters who want to have something sweet can indulge in a cocktail that has fewer calories or carbs than a similarly named dessert. And the meal you've just eaten prevents you from imbibing on an empty stomach, even though after-dinner cocktails don't have to be alcoholic. Smartinis are charming and delightful to the palate, and are offered here in various forms to seduce your taste buds.

Liquid Assets: Stocking Your Bar

You don't have to have every type of liquor that books recommend you buy to have a "complete" bar; you don't even have to buy the liquors on the list to have a "starter" bar. You don't even need to have a bar! As long as you have the space to store your bottles, you can buy what you want and need. A cupboard or shelf plus space in the refrigerator are all you need to be a cocktail-ista. Use the freezer for vodkas and some liqueurs, and the refrigerator for cream-based liqueurs and others that need to be chilled.

For the bare minimum, start out with a "plus" bar. This means you have one item that you add to—for example, choose a liqueur that you add to a mixer, such as an Irish cream liqueur. Your mixers could include coffee, milk, cream, ice cream, or hot chocolate (and most liqueurs can be served plain or on the rocks as well). Whatever you do, buy the best you can afford. It will make a huge difference in how you enjoy what's in your glass, and your friends are worth it.

To make the dessert drinks in this book (and to best experiment with making your own concoctions), follow these suggestions for liquors, rims, garnishes, and add-ins, and stock your bar with your favorites.

Dessert Drink Liquors

Almond liqueur • Banana liqueur • Brandy (plain, apricot, cherry, etc.) • Cherry-flavored liquors (whiskey, cherry advocaat) • Coffee liqueur, coffee brandy • Crème de cacao (chocolate liqueur—white or dark) • Crème de cassis • Crème de menthe (white or green) • Hazelnut liqueur • Irish cream liqueur • Melon liqueur • Orange liqueur (triple sec, Cointreau, Curaçao) • Peach liqueur • Raspberry liqueur • Rum (light, dark, coconut, mango, etc.) • Schnapps (butterscotch, cinnamon, apple, peach, strawberry, etc.) • Vodkas, plain and flavored (vanilla, black currant, lemon, cherry, citrus, etc.)

Rims and Garnishes

Caramel sauce • Chocolate cookie crumbs • Chocolate syrup • Cocoa powder (unsweetened baking cocoa) • Coconut flakes (sweetened or unsweetened) • Fresh fruit (berries, lemons, limes, cherries, oranges, bananas, melons, etc.) • Graham cracker crumbs • Grenadine • Ground nuts (almonds, pecans, etc.) • Hard candies, crushed (peppermints, etc.) • Honey • Instant coffee powder, crushed • Maraschino cherries • Mint sprigs • Shaved or curled chocolate (sweetened, semisweet, etc.) • Spices [cinnamon (ground and sticks), ground nutmeg, cardamom, cloves (ground or whole)] • Sugar (granulated, turbinado, colored, sparkly, etc.) • Vanilla wafer crumbs • Whipped cream

Mixers and Add-ins

Brewed coffee • Fruit juices (pomegranate, cranberry, orange, pineapple, passion fruit, apple, mango) • Cream (half-and-half, heavy cream) • Hot chocolate • Ice • Ice cream • Lime juice (preferably Rose's) • Milk (whole, low fat, skim) • Sodas (cola, lemon-lime, soda water, etc.) • Sour mix • Sugar syrup • Champagne • Espresso

Gourds and Chalices: Glassware You Want

There is a certain charm in using canning jars for your drinks, but that charm can wear thin when guests expect glamorous champagne or an after-dinner cocktail and are handed a clunky jug instead. Some people who entertain friends often may wish to invest in expensive and trendy glassware, but if you aren't up for spending megabucks on fancy stemware, you might luck out at the second-hand store with some mismatched classics. If you need to, you can rent glasses at party supply stores or through catering companies.

Here's a short list of a few you should keep on hand:

- **Brandy snifter** (10 to 18 ounces): Held between the fingers with the bowl in the palm to warm the brandy, this glass is beautifully shaped and perfect to display large dessert drinks.
- **Champagne flutes** (5 to 8 ounces): Tall and thin, these are perfect for bubbly drinks.
- **Champagne saucers** (5 to 8 ounces): These glasses are round and flat, and can be used for frozen, creamy, or blended drinks.
- **Collins glasses** (8 to 16 ounces): Thinner than highball glasses, these narrow, tall glasses are used for cold soda, fruit, or mixed drinks that don't require much ice.
- **Highball glasses** (8 to 12 ounces): Use these vessels for tall and "on the rocks" drinks.
- **Irish coffee glasses** (8 to 9 ounces): The handles on these keep hot beverages from burning your hand.
- **Margarita glass** (8 to 10 ounces): This big-bottomed, rounded glass has a broad rim for salt to stick to, and is also used for frozen fruit and tropical drinks, as well as daiquiris.
- **Martini or cocktail glasses** (3 to 6 ounces): These glasses are specially shaped to prevent mixed drinks from separating, with a stem to keep the warmth of your hand from transferring to the cold drink. Chill before using.
- **Old fashioned glasses** (4 to 8 ounces): A short round glass perfect for cocktails or liquor served "on the rocks".
- **Parfait or hurricane glasses** (about 12 ounces): With a deep bowl and steep rim, these glasses suit frozen drinks, fruit drinks, and ice cream.
- **Shot glasses** (1 to 2 ounces): These are great for measuring liquors and also for serving shooters.
- **Wine glasses** (4 to 8 ounces): Choose white or red or both, depending on what you are serving or what you have on hand.

Broads and Booze:
Women and the Alcoholic Beverage Through the Ages

Alcohol has been an important part of human history—no matter the era, culture, or country—since before recorded history. And it didn't originate as just a way to get tipsy; it was often a means for getting much-needed nutrients, and sometimes played a large part in religion. Rich ancient Egyptians drank wine, while everyone else drank beer. Egyptian religious festivals involved much alcohol, as their gods were believed to enjoy watching their worshippers having a good time. Greek males had formal drinking parties with other men in their richly-furnished dining areas, socializing while reclining on couches. The Romans drank warm, cheap wine in the streets, but the wealthy drank homemade rose wine made with flowers from their prized gardens. It was the Romans who started the custom of men drinking to the health of women: one drink to each letter of their names. During the time of the Spanish Inquisition, wealthy citizens of Seville entertained in salons where the sexes were separated by a wooden screen as women drank rarely and men in moderation. Elizabethan times saw everyone, including children, drinking ale, mead, and cider. The coffee houses in London of the 1650s became gossip traps where men drank, argued politics, gambled, and showed off their trendy new wigs. Around the same time in Russia, people drank their vodka in taverns that served only alcohol, no food.

But women, it seems, preferred to avoid drinking altogether (or conceal their drinking and do so only in private). They could enjoy wine with a meal or take Communion, but they could not consume hard liquor or visit taverns unless they were whores, wives, or servers. There were even separate doors for women to enter. At the end of the nineteenth century, a law was passed in Canada that prohibited women not only from selling liquor, but from working in pubs. And we all remember cranky Civil War heroine, Scarlett O'Hara, drinking in secret and rinsing her mouth with perfume to keep from being found out. There was a huge social stigma attached to women who indulged in drink, based on their reputation as the "weaker sex," a belief that men also pressed upon women as a way to continue to keep them subjugated.

In recent history, women's most important role in the life of alcohol was trying to get it banned. What began as a quest for moderation soon grew into the formation of temperance groups throughout North America. Women had noticed that their husbands beat them more often when they were drunk, and wanted to put an end to that as well as the huge drain on family finances that heavy drinking caused. In the mid-1800s though, it was decided that the only way to stop alcohol abuse was to keep everyone from getting to their drink. Citing religion as their platform, women began doing everything from visiting bars and smashing liquor bottles with hatchets to using their children as cute, singing propaganda machines, holding rollicking public protests, and staging outdoor rallies.

At first, women didn't get very far with their movement. They couldn't vote and as such were considered by the male politicians to not be worth the time to support. Men were the ones doing the drinking and the voting, and no one wanted to risk alienating them. Gals who joined the temperance movement adopted the mantra of "lips that touch liquor will never touch mine," which didn't mean a lot to anyone unless the woman was single and looking to avoid marriage. On the other hand, getting political about something allowed women a chance to assert themselves while still being socially acceptable. They could join a public debate and voice an opinion during a time when women weren't allowed to vote, wear pants, or work outside the home after marriage.

Eventually, politicians eagerly jumped on the cause that so many upper and middle class people supported. As a result, most of North America ended up "dry"—alcohol was illegal to create or sell. That didn't mean people stopped making, drinking, or selling drinks though. In fact it was the naughtiness of sipping prohibited booze that appealed to many of the young people of the time. And there were ways around the law as well, such as getting prescriptions from your doctor for whiskey, patent medicines (which were basically alcohol flavored with herbs and color claiming to solve all of your physical troubles), and underground speakeasies, where you could sneak in to pay top dollar for a sip of the good stuff.

Into the 1920s, Prohibition ended up being a good idea gone bad. People were being poisoned, paralyzed, or killed from the creation or ingestion of homemade alcohol; the mob was doing even more of what the mob does; and because illegal alcohol was so widespread and policing it so costly, Prohibition proved to be unenforceable.

In the end, it all came to some good. Prohibition was repealed in many parts of the United States and Canada by 1933; the mandatory teaching of temperance in schools by Mary Hunt in the early 1900s is the basis for our current anti-drug promotion for kids; and we can drink delicious dessert cocktails and not bathtub gin. In fact, it's been said that the addition of delicious flavorings, juices, and mixers that you'll find in today's popular cocktails were an attempt to cover up the less-than-appealing results of homemade alcohol. Who would have thought that such an anti-drinking frenzy could have brought us such delicious cocktail recipes?

The Upswing of Swanktabulous Cocktail Culture

The huge popularity of the cocktail came at a time when prepackaged, bland convenience foods were being introduced to a generation of housewives who wanted more time to themselves. Vacuums, washing machines, and electric appliances were widely used and cut back on time spent doing the boring stuff. After all the housework was done, the family was fed, and the little ones were tucked snuggly into their beds, Mom and Dad could join the Woodmans in the living room for a few nibbles, a television show or card game, and some cocktails.

> "Eat, drink, and be merry...for tomorrow we may be radioactive."
> *~1950s toast*

The music and films of the time popularized the hip, swanky style of drinks and cigarettes with friends (although I doubt many front parlors had people with Manhattans doing synchronized dancing and breaking into harmonized song). Otherworldly furniture, cheesy jokes about being sloshed, and kitschy cocktail glasses, aprons, napkins, and stirrers took everyone's minds off the backyard bomb shelter and what the president was up to. Being deprived of so much through Prohibition, the Depression, and World War II—and facing the threat of an atomic war—people decided it was time for some fun and indulgence. Cocktail culture fit the bill splendidly.

Liquor companies took the opportunity to advertise their goods. They used catchy slogans and beautiful women drinking fascinating products with trendy names like the Sidecar. It was all so posh—the epitome of elegance and taste. Good manners were in, although the dance with a lampshade on the head went over pretty well at some parties. The cocktail culture of the times was very romantic and easy for all to imitate.

The love affair lasted on and off up until about the 1980s, when classic cocktails fell very much out of favor and the cool thing to do was order shooters and get wasted as quickly as possible. Drinking games and beer guzzling became trendy. Gone was the conversation, the singing, the dancing, the lounge, the culture. All that seemed to be left was Tom Cruise doing gymnastics with a cocktail shaker, and a legacy of shooters with names so naughty you risked a punch in the face if you mistook a fellow patron for the bartender.

Into the new millennium, cocktails are again enjoying a popular resurgence. The original classics are being served (with fewer tacky plastic accompaniments) alongside exciting and interesting new beverages designed by cult bartenders and celebrity chefs around the world. Celebrities casually name-drop their favorite cocktails in movies, television shows, and live interviews as if discussing their famous friends; and by design, that celebrity has instantly associated their name with the drink, firmly entrenching themselves and the cocktail in pop culture. And unlike the cocktails of the past, the rules of making drinks are all broken. Recipes are meant to be individualized and made "to taste" by upping the ratio of one ingredient and reducing another, depending on your own wants. Cutting back on the booze and making mocktails is perfectly acceptable, as is modifying your drink to be low-carb. But don't skimp if you don't have to. It's the simple but luscious decadence of these dessert drinks that make them such a heavenly bit of after-food delight.

A Word about Drinking Responsibly
(You knew this was coming)
I'm a huge fan of decadence. Who isn't? But with cocktails, as with most treats, a little goes a long way. You'll find that lushness is always in vogue, but being a lush…not so much. Enjoy your indulgences responsibly.

Chocolate Indulgence

Can you imagine many things more temptingly delicious than chocolate? A favorite of dessert lovers everywhere, chocolate translates just as well into dessert cocktails. Choose chocolate dessert drinks when you want to impress dinner guests or desire a treat to indulge in.

Chocolate Raspberry Brownie

Chocolate and black raspberry flavors blend exquisitely with coffee liqueur to create a dark, delicious, and decadent midnight treat.

SERVES 1

1 ounce coffee liqueur
1 ounce black raspberry liqueur
1/2 ounce dark crème de cacao
2 ounces cream

1. Chill a martini glass, then fill it with ice.
2. Add the three liqueurs to the glass and follow with the cream. Stir and serve.

Serve in Chilled martini glass

Rim Instant coffee powder, unsweetened cocoa powder, chocolate cake mix

Garnish Skewered raspberries, shaved chocolate

Using a chilled block of your favorite chocolate, make shavings by scraping down the sides with a potato peeler. Store extra chocolate shavings in a sealed container in the refrigerator or freezer.

Death by Chocolate

A more exquisite death couldn't be dreamed of! Enjoy this indulgent drink with shortbread, angel food cake, or fresh fruit such as strawberries, which will intensify the chocolate experience.

SERVES 1

1 ounce dark crème de cacao
1 ounce coffee liqueur
3 ounces heavy cream
1 ounce Tia Maria

Shake all the ingredients in a cocktail shaker half-filled with ice until well chilled. Strain into a chilled glass and serve.

Serve in   Chilled martini glass

Rim   Chocolate cookie crumbs, shaved chocolate, unsweetened cocoa powder, instant coffee powder

Garnish   Chocolate shavings, chocolate candy orange section (such as Terry's Chocolate Orange), fresh fruit

Garnish liberally with chocolate shavings. You may also choose to increase the crème de cacao or the coffee liqueur to 2 ounces and omit the Tia Maria.

Chocolate-Dipped Strawberry

These two classic dessert flavors—chocolate and strawberry—are destined to delight your after-dinner diners! Chill your martini glasses by placing them in the freezer for several minutes before you fill them.

SERVES 1

2 ounces strawberry schnapps
1/2 ounce white crème de cacao
1 ounce cream

Shake all the ingredients in a cocktail shaker half-filled with shaved ice. Strain into a glass half-filled with ice and serve.

Serve in	Chilled martini glass or wine glass
Rim	Unsweetened cocoa powder, chocolate cookie crumbs
Garnish	Chocolate shavings, fresh strawberry (whole or sliced)

Substitute dark crème de cacao if desired. You may also choose to increase the crème de cacao and omit the half-and-half.

Smartini Tip
Instead of strawberry schnapps, use strawberry soda and substitute 1 tablespoon chocolate syrup for the crème de cacao.

Toblerone

This is a scrumptious but simple dessert drink to impress your guests—or dazzle a date. Drizzle the chocolate syrup in a wacky lattice pattern to tempt the eye before you thrill the palate.

SERVES 1

1 teaspoon chocolate syrup
1 ounce Irish cream liqueur
1 ounce hazelnut liqueur
1/2 ounce dark crème de cacao
1 tablespoon honey
1 ounce heavy cream
1/2 cup crushed ice

1. Drizzle the chocolate syrup around the inside of a chilled martini or hurricane glass.

2. In a blender, combine the remaining six ingredients and blend until creamy. Pour into the chocolate-drizzled glass and serve with a straw or spoon.

An extra drizzle of honey over the top of the finished drink is delicious!

Serve in	Chilled martini glass, hurricane glass
Rim	Unsweetened cocoa powder, chocolate cookie crumbs
Garnish	Chocolate sprinkles, chocolate shavings, ground almonds

Chocolate Caramel Martini

As tasty as a caramel-coated brownie, this chilled sipper lasts longer! You can also offer your dinner guests the butterscotch schnapps straight, in regular or iced coffee, or poured over ice cream.

SERVES 1

3/4 ounce vodka
3/4 ounce Irish cream liqueur
1/2 ounce coffee liqueur
1 ounce chocolate liqueur
1 ounce butterscotch schnapps

Shake all the ingredients in a cocktail shaker half-filled with ice until well chilled. Strain into a chilled glass and serve.

Crème de cacao is also known as chocolate liqueur and comes in many different varieties: clear, white, dark, creamy. Use your favorite brand, or experiment with what you have available.

Serve in	Chilled martini glass
Rim	Chocolate cake mix, unsweetened cocoa powder, instant coffee powder
Garnish	Chocolate shavings, unsweetened cocoa powder, coffee beans

Chocolate Toasted Almond

Chocolate and toasted almonds are a popular candy bar combo. You can add a toasted almond rim to this drink by placing a single layer of finely ground almonds on a baking sheet and baking for a few minutes in a 350°F oven until lightly browned. To make the nuts stick, try dipping the rim in thinned sugar syrup.

SERVES 1

1 ounce coffee liqueur
1 ounce almond liqueur
8 ounces milk
2 tablespoons chocolate syrup

Shake all the ingredients in a cocktail shaker half-filled with ice until well chilled. Strain into a chilled glass and serve.

Serve in	Chilled martini glass or Collins glass
Rim	Toasted ground almonds, unsweetened cocoa powder, instant coffee powder
Garnish	Toasted ground almonds, ground cinnamon, unsweetened cocoa powder

For a frozen treat, try mixing the drink in a blender and adding ice cream instead of milk. Blend until the mixture is smooth and creamy and serve with a spoon. Or mix the other ingredients without the milk and serve over ice cream.

Frozen Mudslide

The "mudslide" in this frozen drink is created by letting the chocolate syrup drizzle off the spoon into the whipped cream on top. The chocolate "mud" will "slide" down the sides to collect in a delicious puddle!

SERVES 1

1 ounce vodka
1 ounce Irish cream liqueur
1 ounce coffee liqueur
1 cup cracked ice
4 ounces milk
Whipped cream (optional)
1 tablespoon chocolate syrup

1. In a blender, combine the vodka and liqueurs with the cracked ice and blend until smooth.

2. Pour the mixture into a chilled glass and top with the milk; do not mix.

3. Top with whipped cream, if desired, then drizzle the chocolate syrup from a spoon onto the whipped cream so that it collects inside the bottom of the glass. Serve at once.

Serve in	Chilled martini glass, brandy snifter, hurricane glass
Rim	Unsweetened cocoa powder, chocolate cookie crumbs, instant coffee powder
Garnish	Whole fresh strawberry, chocolate shavings, mint leaves

Make a regular mudslide with 1 1/2 ounce Irish cream liqueur, 1/2 ounces coffee liqueur, and chocolate syrup. Drizzle the chocolate syrup around the inside of a frozen glass. Shake the liqueurs in a cocktail shaker half-filled with ice until cold. Strain into the chocolate-drizzled glass and serve.

After-Dinner Mint

A delightful change from the usual after-dinner mint, this version features hot chocolate and mint with the unexpected touch of peach liqueur. Serve it to warm the chilliest heart, even on the coldest day.

SERVES 1

1/2 ounce white crème de menthe
3/4 ounce peach liqueur
1/2 ounce vodka
Hot chocolate
Whipped cream (optional)

1. Shake the liqueurs and vodka in a cocktail shaker without ice.
2. Pour the mixture into an Irish coffee glass or a regular mug and fill with hot chocolate; stir.
3. Top with whipped cream, if desired, and serve.

Substitute green crème de menthe if you don't have the white, and try vanilla-flavored vodka for a slightly different taste.

Serve in	Irish coffee mug or other mug
Rim	None
Garnish	Crushed peppermint candies or candy canes; coarsely chopped chocolate mint candies

Cherries Jubilee

This drink is usually made by cooking cherries in a syrup until it is thickened, then adding alcohol and setting it alight in a darkened room for added drama. The version here gives you all the same flavors, but you'll need a different excuse to turn out the lights.

SERVES 1

1 ounce cherry advocaat
1 ounce white crème de cacao
1/2 ounce coconut rum
2 ounces half-and-half

Shake all the ingredients in a cocktail shaker half-filled with ice until well chilled. Strain in a glass and serve.

Serve in   Martini glass

Rim   Grated chocolate, sweetened coconut flakes

Garnish   Grated chocolate, skewered maraschino cherries

Try cherry whiskey, cherry brandy, or other cherry-flavored liqueurs in place of the cherry advocaat.

Grasshopper

Reminiscent of the pie by the same name, the grasshopper is a tempting sipper combining chocolate and mint. If you have only the white crème de menthe, add a few drops of green food coloring.

SERVES 1

1 ounce green crème de menthe
1 ounce white crème de cacao
1 ounce cream

Shake all the ingredients in a cocktail shaker half-filled with shaved ice until well chilled. Strain into a chilled glass and serve.

Substitute dark crème de cacao if desired.

Serve in	Chilled champagne saucer, martini glass
Rim	Unsweetened cocoa powder, chocolate cookie crumbs, crushed peppermint candies
Garnish	Chocolate shavings or sprinkles, mint leaves, maraschino cherries

German Chocolate Cake

Mixing up and baking a real German chocolate cake can be a complicated and time-consuming experience. This drinkable dessert has all the same flavors, can be made in record time, and doesn't require heating up the stove in summer!

SERVES 1

1 ounce coffee liqueur
1 ounce coconut rum
2 tablespoons chocolate syrup
1 teaspoon pecans
2 scoops vanilla ice cream
Crushed ice

In a blender combine all the ingredients and blend until smooth. Pour over crushed ice in a chilled glass and serve.

Omit the blender and ice and reserve the ice cream. Mix the remaining ingredients in a cocktail shaker, then serve over the ice cream.

Serve in	Hurricane glass
Rim	Ground pecans, unsweetened cocoa powder, chocolate cookie crumbs, sweetened coconut flakes, toasted coconut flakes
Garnish	Crushed nuts, chocolate shavings

Chocolate Martini

A simple-to-make trendsetting sipper, this exquisite martini can be made to your own taste by modifying the ratio of vodka to crème de cacao (for example, increase the crème de cacao to 2 ounces for a stronger chocolate taste). The colder you make this martini, the better it tastes!

SERVES 1

2 ounces vodka
1/2 ounce white crème de cacao

Shake all the ingredients in a cocktail shaker half-filled with ice until well chilled. Strain into a chilled glass and serve.

Serve in   Chilled martini glass
Rim   None
Garnish   Coffee beans or cacao beans

> **Try vanilla vodka, chocolate vodka, or another flavored version for a delicious twist.**

Chocolate Rum

This decadent drink will please even hardcore rum connoisseurs. For a different take on the same idea, try using dark rum or coconut rum instead of the light.

SERVES 1

1 ounce light rum
1/2 ounce dark crème de cacao
1/2 ounce white crème de menthe
1 tablespoon half-and-half

Shake all the ingredients in a cocktail shaker half-filled with ice. Strain into a chilled glass filled with ice and serve.

Add a few tablespoons of chocolate syrup before mixing, then pour over ice cream.

Serve in	Chilled old fashioned glass or martini glass
Rim	None
Garnish	Cherries, fresh or maraschino

Chocolate Black Russian

A chocolate version of the classic Black Russian cocktail, this frozen drink brings a chill to hot days and a divine indulgence to frosty ones.

SERVES 1

1 ounce coffee liqueur
1/2 ounce vodka
5 ounces chocolate ice cream

In a blender combine all the ingredients and process briefly until smooth. Pour into a cold glass and serve.

Serve in	Chilled champagne flute
Rim	None
Garnish	Mint leaves, instant coffee powder

Make a regular Black Russian with 1 1/2 ounces vodka and 3/4 ounce coffee liqueur poured over ice. A White Russian is 1 ounce coffee liqueur with 2 ounces vodka poured over ice and topped with milk or cream, and a Russian is equal parts vodka, gin, and white crème de cacao mixed with ice and strained into a chilled martini glass.

Sweet and Sour Sippers

These lip-smackers combine two of the best dessert tastes: sweet and sour. If you favor one of these over the other, feel free to adjust the recipes to reflect your favorite blend. A scrumptious end to a casual meal, these dessert drinks are captivating and tangy, with an allure of the exotic.

Midori Sour

Sometimes something a little sour is just what your puckered lips desire. The sour melon flavor and soda fizz in this drink make a surprising but very refreshing combination that's perfect for cleansing the palate.

SERVES 1

1 ounce melon liqueur
1 ounce sour mix
2 ounces lemon-lime soda

1. Add ice to a glass, then pour in the liqueur and sour mix; stir.

2. Stir in the soda but only briefly to keep the bubbles. Serve immediately.

Serve in	Chilled highball glass
Rim	Sugar of choice (granulated, colored, etc.)
Garnish	Speared maraschino cherries, fresh lemon and/or lime wedge, skewered chunks of melon

> **Make your own sour mix by dissolving 1 cup sugar in 1 cup each of fresh lemon juice, fresh lime juice, and filtered water. Store in the refrigerator in a sealed bottle.**

Smartini Tip

Omit the melon liqueur and substitute melon juice or punch. If the lemon-lime soda makes the drink too sweet, try substituting club soda or sparkling water instead.

Pomegranate Martini

Oh-so-trendy and a shocking shade of pink, this sweet but tart martini uses fresh pomegranate juice and packs a nutritional punch of antioxidants and potassium.

SERVES 1

1 ounce vodka
1/2 ounce orange liqueur
3 ounces pomegranate juice

Shake all the ingredients in a cocktail shaker half-filled with ice until well chilled. Strain into a chilled glass and serve.

Fresh juice is best, but if you can't get fresh pomegranate juice there are several bottled varieties on the market that are delicious.

Serve in	Chilled martini glass
Rim	None
Garnish	Lemon slice, orange slice

Smartini Tip

Omit the vodka and orange liqueur and substitute 2 ounces freshly squeezed or pulp-free orange juice. Increase the pomegranate juice if desired.

Pink Monsoon

Refreshing any time but especially wonderful on a warm spring day, this drink sparkles with flavor and color. Try club soda or carbonated spring water instead of the lemon-lime soda for a less sweet drink.

SERVES 1

1 ounce vodka
2 ounces cranberry juice
5 ounces lemon-lime soda

1. Shake the vodka and juice in a cocktail shaker half-filled with ice.
2. Strain into a glass filled with ice. Top with the lemon-lime soda, stir gently, and serve.

Add a dash of grenadine or some crème de cacao for an interesting change.

Serve in	Highball glass
Rim	None
Garnish	Lemon wedge, lime wedge

Smartini Tip

Omit the vodka and increase the cranberry juice, trying different flavors of cranberry juices available, such as a cran-raspberry or cran-cherry, for variety.

Cherry Pucker

This drink delivers the luscious taste of cherries, with nary a pit in sight! For a more puckery Cherry Pucker, try slipping in a little sour mix.

SERVES 1

2 ounces cherry brandy
1 ounce almond liqueur
1 ounce vodka
2 ounces cranberry juice
1 lemon twist
1 lime twist

Pour the liquors and juice in a glass half-filled with ice. Add the twists of lemon and lime, stir, and serve.

Serve in	Highball glass
Rim	Ground almonds
Garnish	Skewered cherries (maraschino or fresh), lemon wedge

To make a citrus twist, wash the outside peel of a fresh lemon, lime, or orange. Slice off both ends and along the top of the fruit from one end to the other; scoop out the inside of the fruit with a small spoon. Open up the peel and using a sharp knife, cut quarter-inch pieces. Twist the peel over the drink to release the flavourful oils before dropping it in to the drink; or rub along an ungarnished rim.

Key Lime Pie Martini

This is an absolute hit that is a cinch to prepare! Serve it for a summer patio party, a holiday cocktail event, or even a regular girl's night out.

SERVES 1

2 ounces vanilla vodka
1 ounce pineapple juice
1 ounce melon liqueur
1 teaspoon sour mix
1 teaspoon half-and-half
Whipped cream (optional)

1. Shake all the ingredients in a cocktail shaker half-filled with ice until well chilled. Strain into a chilled glass.

2. Top with whipped cream, if using, and serve.

Serve in   Chilled martini glass
Rim   Crushed graham crackers, crushed vanilla wafers
Garnish   Lime wedge, mint sprig

For a martini that's more tart, use a little more sour mix and reduce the pineapple juice.

After-Dinner Cocktail

This classic after-dinner drink uses apricot-flavored brandy, which is just as delicious sipped on its own. An elegant end to any dinner, this citrus-apricot drink can also be made and served without ice.

SERVES 1

1 ounce triple sec
1 ounce apricot brandy
Juice of 1 medium lime

Shake all the ingredients in a cocktail shaker half-filled with ice until well chilled. Strain into a glass and serve.

Use fresh lime juice, not lime concentrate. One medium lime produces about 1 1/2 teaspoons of juice.

Serve in	Old-fashioned glass
Rim	None
Garnish	Fresh-sliced wedge of lime

Red Sky at Night

They say that a red sky at night is a sailor's delight, but you don't need to be an old salty to enjoy this black currant-flavored refreshment. Make a Kir Royale by substituting champagne for the soda and omitting the lemon.

SERVES 1

1/2 ounce freshly squeezed lemon juice
1 ounce crème de cassis
Lemon-lime soda

1. Chill a glass and fill with ice.

2. Pour in the lemon juice and crème de cassis. Top with lemon-lime soda, stir gently, and serve.

Serve in	Highball or Collins glass
Rim	Crushed graham crackers, crushed vanilla wafers
Garnish	Lemon slice, skewered strawberries

> **To make a lemon easier to juice, allow it to reach room temperature and then roll the fruit, with a firm pressure, on the counter with your palm.**

Smartini Tip
Omit the black currant liqueur and substitute 1 tablespoon black currant syrup, which is available in supermarkets in the beverage section or imported foods section.

Cranapple Martini

The cranapple martini may just become your next holiday favorite! A festive and enticing drink worth celebrating by itself, it is a perfect conclusion to any Thanksgiving or Christmas feast.

SERVES 1

1 ounce vodka
1 1/2 ounces sour apple schnapps
Cranberry juice

1. Shake the vodka and schnapps in a cocktail shaker half-filled with ice until well chilled.
2. Strain into a glass, fill with cranberry juice, and serve.

Serve in	Martini glass
Rim	None
Garnish	Mint sprigs, orange slice, apple slice

Try various blends of cranberry juices to get the most pleasing sweet and sour combination you like.

Moonlight Cocktail

There are fewer things in this world more enchanting than the moon. Enjoy this cocktail under the stars with your friends and loved ones.

SERVES 1

2 ounces brandy
Juice of 1 medium lemon
1 teaspoon confectioners' sugar

Shake all the ingredients in cocktail shaker half-filled with ice. Strain into a glass with ice and serve.

Substitute sugar syrup for confectioners' sugar. Make the syrup by dissolving 2 cups sugar in 2 cups boiling water. Allow the mixture to cool, then store in the refrigerator. Also, 1 medium lemon will give you about 3 tablespoons of juice, which is about 1 1/2 ounces (45 milliliters).

Serve in	Old fashioned glass or martini glass
Rim	None
Garnish	Lemon wedge, lemon twist

Lemon Meringue Pie

This lemon meringue pie martini recipe removes the worry over burned crusts, weeping tops, and sloshy filling! Plus, you're left with only glasses to clean instead of all those plates and forks.

SERVES 1

2 ounces lemon vodka
1 ounce Drambuie
1 ounce freshly squeezed lemon juice
1 teaspoon sugar syrup (page 42)

Shake all the ingredients in a cocktail shaker half-filled with ice until foamy. Strain into a chilled glass and serve.

Serve in   Chilled martini glass or margarita glass

Rim   Sugar of choice (granulated, colored, etc.)

Garnish   Lemon twist

Add a splash of sour mix to give this drink a much more tart lemon flavor.

Flirty Liqueurs

Sweet, sensual, and pampering, liqueurs are delicious and very versatile. Make your favorites into the following recipes; then try new liqueurs and see what you can come up with. Liqueurs can be served chilled and on their own, and you can also use them to marinate mashed berries or other fruit for serving over cake or ice cream.

After Eight

*Imagine the distinctive taste of the creamy, minty, chocolate wafers in a tempting sipper!
Perfect for any occasion but a special treat after a festive dinner, this drink will even
delight guests who think they ate too much.*

SERVES 1

1/2 ounce coffee-flavored liqueur
3/4 ounce Irish cream liqueur
1/2 ounce green crème de menthe
1/2 ounce chocolate liqueur

Add all the ingredients to a tall cordial glass, stir, and serve.

Serve in   Cordial glass
Rim   Unsweetened cocoa powder
Garnish   Crushed peppermint candies, chocolate
shavings, coarsely chopped chocolate mints

**Try adding cream or milk
for a smoother sipper. And
if green crème de menthe
is not available, use white.
There is no difference in
taste between the two.**

Boston Cream Pie

Vanilla-flavored vodka gives the perfect balance to this drinkable dessert, reminiscent of the classic cake and custard with chocolate. While the baked version takes a skilled hand, the beverage is a no-brainer and requires no slicing.

SERVES 1

1 1/2 ounces vanilla vodka
1 1/2 ounces chocolate liqueur
1 1/2 ounces Irish cream liqueur
3 tablespoons unsweetened cocoa powder

Shake all the ingredients in a cocktail shaker half-filled with ice until well chilled. Strain into a chilled glass and serve.

Serve in	Chilled margarita glass or martini glass
Rim	Unsweetened cocoa powder, sugar of choice (granulated, colored, etc.), chocolate cake mix, graham cracker crumbs, vanilla wafer crumbs
Garnish	Chocolate shavings

If you do feel like doing a little baking, serve this yummy drink with a slice of plain yellow cake.

Pretty Woman

Sing the lyrics to the famous Roy Orbison song with your friends while you blend this, and you'll be sipping pretty in no time.

SERVES 1

Melon mixture:
1 ounce melon liqueur
1 ounce coconut rum
1/2 cup ice

Strawberry mixture:
1 ounce strawberry liqueur
5 fresh or frozen whole strawberries, hulled
1/2 cup ice

1. In a blender combine the melon mixture's ingredients and blend until smooth. Pour into a small bowl and set aside.

2. Rinse the blender and blades thoroughly, then blend the strawberry liqueur, 4 strawberries, and the ice until smooth. Pour into a small bowl and set aside.

3. Tilt a chilled hurricane (or other tall) glass and add half of the melon mixture. Tilt it another way and add half of the strawberry mixture. Continue until there is no remaining mixtures.

4. Garnish with the remaining strawberry on the side of the glass and serve.

> **You can use a hand held blender or stationary blender when making this drink.**

Serve in	Chilled hurricane glass
Rim	Sweetened coconut flakes
Garnish	Whole strawberries, skewered melon chunks or melon balls

Smartini Tip
Substitute melon juice for the melon liqueur, 1/2 teaspoon coconut extract for coconut rum, and omit strawberry liqueur.

Caramel Apple Martini

Enjoy this delicious drink with your soul mate without the fear of any chewy caramel sticking your teeth together. Simple to prepare, it goes down easy and will remind you of trick-or-treating with friends.

SERVES 1

2 ounces apple rum
2 ounces butterscotch schnapps

Shake all ingredients in a cocktail shaker half-filled with ice until well chilled. Strain into a glass and serve.

Serve in	Martini glass
Rim	None
Garnish	Apple slices

Try the apple rum with cinnamon schnapps for a Candy Apple delicacy, or use sour apple liqueur for a tart Caramel Granny treat.

Sheer Elegance

The obvious style and magnificence of this drink's almond and raspberry liqueurs is grace in a glass. Relish after a sumptuous dinner or when the mood strikes to indulge in something luxurious.

SERVES 1

1 1/2 ounces almond liqueur
1 1/2 ounces raspberry liqueur
1/2 ounce vodka

Shake all the ingredients in a cocktail shaker half-filled with ice until well chilled. Strain into a chilled glass and serve immediately.

Experiment with other flavored vodkas, such as vanilla and raspberry, and discover other taste sensations that are as equally elegant.

Serve in	Chilled martini glass
Rim	None
Garnish	Individual or skewered raspberries

Black Currant Trifle

When it comes to after-dinner and late-night indulgences, the darker the better! Black currant and rich, ripe raspberries mixed with cream can soothe any midnight beasties.

SERVES 1

1 ounce black currant vodka
1 ounce raspberry liqueur
1 ounce Irish cream liqueur
Milk or cream

1. Shake the vodka and liqueurs in a cocktail shaker half-filled with ice until well chilled.

2. Strain into a chilled glass, top with milk, stir, and serve.

Serve in	Chilled martini glass
Rim	None
Garnish	Skewered raspberries

Serve with unfrosted white or yellow cake for a nice accompaniment.

Jam Doughnut and Coffee

Here are three flavors that save you from popping out to the local doughnut hangout for fried tidbits and a hot cup o' joe: raspberry, coffee, and cream. Substitute another favorite liqueur to match your choice of doughnut flavor.

Serves 1

1 ounce Irish cream liqueur
1 ounce coffee liqueur
1 ounce raspberry liqueur

Shake all the ingredients in a cocktail shaker half-filled with ice until well chilled. Strain into a chilled glass and serve.

Serve in	Chilled martini glass
Rim	Instant coffee powder, unsweetened cocoa powder
Garnish	Individual or skewered raspberries

You may also try adding in some crème de cacao for some chocolate flair (which is always a great addition to any doughnut). If you prefer a creamy drink, top with milk or cream after pouring into the glass.

Bedtime Bouncer

Mom always said, "Don't play ball in the house," but this drink is made more for mattress jumping. Besides, what mom doesn't know won't hurt her.

SERVES 1

2 ounces brandy
1 ounce triple sec
1 orange twist

1. Shake the brandy and triple sec in a cocktail shaker half-filled with ice until well chilled.

2. Strain into a chilled glass, then stir in the orange twist before serving.

Chill the martini glass by placing it in the freezer for several minutes before pouring in the beverage. You can also twist the orange peel over the drink before adding as a garnish to release the tasty oils into the drink.

Serve in	Chilled martini glass
Rim	None
Garnish	Orange twist

Spice Cake

Tempting liqueurs combine to create a spice cake replica that will entice your dinner guests after holiday meals. Serve this drink with fresh strawberries and saucers of brown sugar and cream cheese to dip the fruit into for a truly decadent after-dinner treat.

SERVES 1

1 ounce Irish cream liqueur
1 ounce almond liqueur
1 ounce cinnamon schnapps

Shake all the ingredients in a cocktail shaker half-filled with ice. Strain into a chilled glass filled with ice and serve.

Serve in	Chilled martini glass
Rim	Spice cake mix, ground almonds, ground cinnamon
Garnish	Skewered strawberries, ground cinnamon

For a Cupcake Martini, add 2 ounces vanilla vodka to a martini glass and fill with lemon-lime soda.

Cream and Sugar Charmers

An elegant end to any dinner, these creamy delicacies convey class and comfort with velvety lushness. Although some recipe books sometimes specify the type of cream felt to be best suited for the drink, experiment with what your own tastes dictate—using milks and creams of your choice, from heavy to light.

Toasted Almond

The smell of roasting almonds is enough to make your mouth water; tasting the result is even better! Two other versions of this recipe are included in the tip if you prefer the darker taste of burnt almond flavors.

SERVES 1

2 ounces almond liqueur
2 ounces coffee liqueur
2 ounces half-and-half

Shake all the ingredients in a cocktail shaker half-filled with ice until well chilled. Strain into a glass and serve.

Serve in	Highball glass
Rim	Ground almonds (toasted or untoasted), instant coffee powder
Garnish	Ground almonds (toasted or untoasted), ground cinnamon

To make a Burnt Almond, mix 1/2 ounce almond liqueur, 1/2 ounce white crème de cacao, and 1/2 ounce coffee liqueur with milk. To make a Burnt Toasted Almond, combine 1/2 ounce vodka with 3/4 ounce coffee liqueur and 3/4 ounce almond liqueur with half-and-half.

Banana Cream Pie

This is a classic dessert that is equally decadent as a dessert drink. Serve with chocolate of any kind: squares, brownies, cake, ice cream, or truffles.

SERVES 1

1 ounce banana liqueur
1 ounce dark crème de cacao
1 ounce vodka
1 ounce half-and-half

Shake all the ingredients in a cocktail shaker half-filled with ice until well chilled. Strain into chilled glass and serve.

Serve in	Chilled martini glass
Rim	Coconut flakes (sweetened or unsweetened), unsweetened cocoa powder
Garnish	Ground cinnamon, whipped cream

Turn it up a notch by adding coconut rum or rum extract.

Brandy Alexander

The ratios may change, but everyone seems to agree: the Brandy Alexander is the ideal after-dinner drink. Brandy by itself is also a nice nightcap, poured into a snifter and warmed by the hand cradling it.

SERVES 1

1 1/2 ounces brandy
1 ounce dark crème de cacao
1 ounce cream

Shake all the ingredients in a cocktail shaker half-filled with ice until well chilled. Strain into a chilled glass and serve at once.

Serve in	Chilled martini glass
Rim	None
Garnish	Grated nutmeg

Made with gin and popular in the 1950s, the Alexander is 2 ounces gin, 1 ounce crème de cacao, and 1 ounce cream dusted with nutmeg.

Smartini Tip

Alexander's Daughter is a nonalcoholic version made with 1 ounce chocolate syrup, 1 ounce ginger syrup, and 1 ounce cream dusted with nutmeg.

Dreamy Monkey

Containing exactly what you'd imagine it would—banana and chocolate—this creamy frozen drink adds ice cream to excite and delight. Choose a different ice cream flavor if you wish, as vanilla is not the only flavor that works well with this drink.

SERVES 1

1 ounce vodka
1/2 ounce crème de bananas
1/2 ounce dark crème de cacao
1/2 medium banana, peeled
2 scoops vanilla ice cream
1 ounce half-and-half

In a blender combine all the ingredients and blend until smooth. Pour into a chilled glass and serve.

Try vanilla vodka or chocolate vodka instead of plain vodka. Also remember to use fairly ripe and well-speckled bananas for blended drinks. For garnishes a bold yellow banana with firm fruit works best.

Serve in	Chilled parfait glass
Rim	Unsweetened cocoa powder, chocolate shavings, chocolate cake mix
Garnish	Whipped cream, shaved chocolate, remaining banana half

Smartini Tip

Omit the vodka and liqueurs, then substitute 2 tablespoons chocolate syrup and another ounce of cream. Use the whole banana in the mix and add banana extract if you desire extra monkey flavor.

Nutty Irishman

When it comes to hazelnut dessert drinks, the nuttier the better. Feel free to alter the ratios of the liqueurs to find the combination of flavors that best suit you and your guests.

SERVES 1

1 ounce hazelnut liqueur
1 ounce Irish cream liqueur
1 ounce cream

Shake all the ingredients in a cocktail shaker half-filled with ice until well chilled. Strain into a chilled glass and serve.

Serve in	Chilled martini glass
Rim	None
Garnish	Grated nutmeg, chocolate flakes

For a lighter drink, try milk instead of cream, or omit the cream and add 1/2 ounce fresh lime juice.

Silk Stockings

When World War II broke out, women found themselves first without silk stockings and then without any at all (nylon was used to make things such as parachutes). These days, no woman needs to go without the little extras in life, especially if you have the ingredients for this silky cocktail on hand.

SERVES 1

1 1/2 ounces tequila
1/2 ounce dark crème de cacao
1 ounce heavy cream
1/2 ounce raspberry liqueur

Shake all the ingredients in a cocktail shaker half-filled with ice until well chilled. Strain into a chilled glass and serve.

Serve in	Chilled martini glass
Rim	Skewered raspberries
Garnish	Ground cinnamon

If you aren't a fan of tequila, substitute coconut rum or coffee liqueur for something different and equally delicious.

Lover's Kiss

A first kiss is always the sweetest. This Lover's Kiss cocktail is not as sweet but is definitely as welcomed. Cheery cherry and indulgent almond make a lush dessert drink that will please even finicky diners.

SERVES 1

1/2 ounce almond liqueur
1/2 ounce cherry brandy
1/2 ounce dark crème de cacao
1 ounce cream
Whipped cream (optional)

1. Shake the liqueurs and cream in a cocktail shaker half-filled with ice until well chilled.

2. Strain into a glass. Top with whipped cream, if desired, and serve.

Serve in	Parfait glass
Rim	Chocolate shavings
Garnish	Chocolate shavings, maraschino cherries, ground almonds

Increase the crème de cacao for a more chocolaty kiss.

Coffee Crisp

Three decadent tastes combine for a divine drink to toast the evening meal. Serve without milk for a stronger sipper or use cream for a smoother one.

SERVES 1

1/2 ounce almond liqueur
1/2 ounce coffee liqueur
1/2 ounce Irish cream liqueur
Milk

1. Shake the liqueurs in a cocktail shaker with a little ice.

2. Strain into a chilled glass. Top with milk, stir, and serve.

To make rim garnishes stick hold the glass upside down by its stem. Using a wedge of lemon or lime, rub the wet fruit around the rim. Dip the rim into a shallow plate of your rim garnish to coat, and allow to dry.

Serve in	Chilled martini glass
Rim	Ground almonds, instant coffee powder, unsweetened cocoa powder, chocolate shavings
Garnish	Whipped cream, chocolate shavings

Cinnamon Nuts and Cream

Heavenly hazelnut liqueur is delicious by itself; combine it with cinnamon schnapps and almond liqueur and you're in for a treat! It's also a great warmer to chase the chill on a cool autumn day or after shoveling snow.

SERVES 1

1 ounce hazelnut liqueur
1/2 ounce cinnamon schnapps
1/2 ounce almond liqueur
1 ounce cream

1. Shake the liqueurs in a cocktail shaker half-filled with ice.

2. Strain into a chilled glass. Top with the cream and stir. Add ice as desired and serve.

Serve in   Chilled martini glass or old fashioned glass

Rim   Ground nuts (almonds, hazelnuts, or pecans)

Garnish   Ground nuts (almonds, hazelnuts, or pecans), ground cinnamon

Drag out your blender and mix this drink with some ice for a frozen drink that's perfect for summer.

Fruit Fetish

The flavorful burst of fresh fruit flavor invokes memories of summertime, gentle breezes, and sweet juices running down your chin. These after-dinner drinks are easy sippin', tropical reminiscin' refreshments that are perfect finales to a meal, no matter the season.

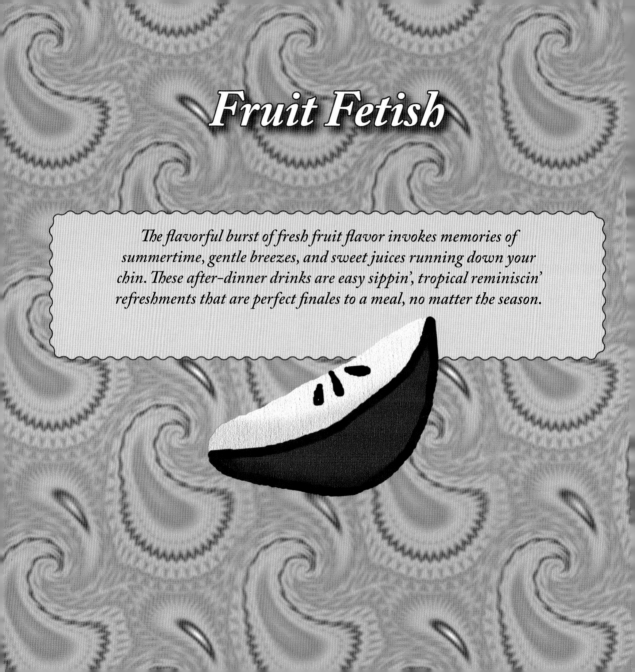

Apple Crumble Martini

This is not your mother's apple crumble! Deliciously inviting yet familiar, it has the name and flavor of a comfortable classic but with the naughtiness of booze.

SERVES 1

1 ounce apple schnapps
1/2 ounce brandy
1/2 ounce Irish cream liqueur

Shake all the ingredients in a cocktail shaker half-filled with ice until well chilled. Strain into a chilled glass and serve.

Serve in	Martini glass
Rim	Graham cracker crumbs, crushed vanilla wafers
Garnish	Graham cracker crumbs, whipped cream, ground cinnamon

Put your blender to good use and add 2 scoops vanilla ice cream and 2 tablespoons graham cracker crumbs with the apple schnapps, brandy, and Irish cream liqueur. Blend until smooth, pour into a parfait glass, top with more graham cracker crumbs, and serve with a spoon.

Pineapple Fizz

Fresh pineapple contains an enzyme called bromelain, which aids in digestion. Enjoy this cocktail with fresh pineapple juice after a hearty summer meal, when something light is desired.

SERVES 1

1 ounce pineapple juice
1/2 teaspoon confectioners' sugar
2 ounces light rum
Club soda

1. Shake the juice, confectioners' sugar, and rum in a cocktail shaker half-filled with ice.

2. Strain into a glass. Top with club soda, add two ice cubes, and serve.

Instead of confectioners' sugar, use sugar syrup (page 42). It dissolves better and delivers a more professional cocktail.

Serve in	Highball glass
Rim	Sugar of choice (granulated, colored, etc.)
Garnish	Sliced pineapple, cut into rounds or wedges

Smartini Tip
Omit the rum and substitute 1/4 teaspoonful rum extract instead.

Apple Granny Crisp

Comforting and familiar, this recipe has no crunch to distract you from your guests and what they have to say. A comforting end to any meal, try serving this one after any traditional holiday meal throughout the year.

SERVES 1

1 ounce apple schnapps
1/2 ounce brandy
1/2 ounce Irish cream liqueur
2 scoops vanilla ice cream
2 tablespoons graham cracker crumbs

In a blender, combine all the ingredients and blend until smooth. Pour into a glass and serve.

Serve in   Parfait glass

Rim   Ground dry oats, ground almonds or nuts, graham cracker crumbs, vanilla wafer crumbs

Garnish   Whipped cream, ground cinnamon, graham cracker crumbs

Try sour apple liqueur or a little sour mix for a real green apple taste.

Passionate Peach Fizz

Peach and passion fruit are a seductive pairing perfect for an after-dinner drink. If you have fresh fruit on hand, mix chunks of the fruit with the peach schnapps and some ice in the blender for a frozen version.

SERVES 1

2 ounces fresh orange juice
2 ounces passion fruit juice
1/2 ounce peach schnapps
Champagne or sparkling wine

1. Shake the juices and schnapps in a cocktail shaker half-filled with ice until well chilled.
2. Strain into a glass, top with Champagne, and serve.

Experiment with the ratios of orange and passion fruit juices to find what you like the most. Also, you may wish to try a splash of cinnamon or almond liqueur.

Serve in	Champagne flute or saucer
Rim	None
Garnish	Peach or nectarine slice or skewered slices

Smartini Tip
Omit the peach schnapps and add peach juice, then substitute ginger ale, lemon-lime soda, or sparkling water for the Champagne.

Midnight Martini

Why wait until the new day begins to clink glasses with this simple and chic cocktail?
Serve the midnight martini when the mood strikes, not when the clock does.

1 ounce apricot brandy
1/2 ounce triple sec
1 tablespoon freshly squeezed lemon juice

Shake all the ingredients in a cocktail shaker half-filled with ice until well chilled. Strain into a glass and serve.

Serve in	Martini glass
Rim	None
Garnish	None

Substitute freshly squeezed orange juice for the lemon to create a less tangy version.

Soother Cocktail

The velvet magic of this cocktail is soothing as well as smoothing. Serve it after a late dinner to enjoy some quiet time with friends, family, or a loved one.

SERVES 1

1/2 ounce brandy
1/2 ounce apple brandy
1/2 ounce triple sec
Juice of 1/2 medium lemon
1 teaspoon confectioners' sugar

Shake all the ingredients in a cocktail shaker half-filled with ice until well chilled. Strain into a glass, and serve.

Serve in	Martini glass
Rim	None
Garnish	Lemon slice, lemon twist

Use sugar syrup (page 42) instead of the confectioners' sugar so that you don't take away from the velvet magic of this cocktail.

Blueberry Cheesecake

A darker but equally delicious dessert, this blueberry cheesecake drink uses yogurt and advocaat to smooth out the wrinkles in your day. Celebrate or commiserate with this cocktail, or save it for a night of passion.

SERVES 1

2 teaspoons blueberry jelly
6 ounces lemon yogurt or vanilla yogurt
2 ounces advocaat
1 ounce lemon vodka

1. Place the blueberry jelly in the bottom of a chilled glass and set aside.

2. Shake the yogurt, advocaat, and vodka in a cocktail shaker one-quarter full of ice.

3. Strain the mixture into the glass to cover the jelly and serve.

Serve in	Chilled parfait glass or martini glass
Rim	Crushed graham cracker crumbs
Garnish	Lemon twist

Try different flavors of yogurt, such as coffee or strawberry, to add some variety. Blueberry schnapps or another fruit liqueur can be an interesting replacement for the lemon vodka, and your local grocer's shelves offer other kinds of jelly to substitute for the blueberry jelly. Experiment, and enjoy the science!

Black and White Cherry

The black and white in this frozen cocktail is chocolate, combined with cherry, vanilla, and cream to deliver memories of summertime as a kid.

SERVES 1

1 ounce dark chocolate liqueur
1 ounce white chocolate liqueur
1 ounce heavy cream
1 ounce cherry vodka
1 ounce vanilla vodka
2 scoops chocolate ice cream
A dozen ice cubes

In a blender combine all the ingredients and blend until creamy and smooth. Pour into a large glass and serve.

If you wish to ditch the blender, mix the alcohol and cream with ice in a cocktail shaker, then strain the mixture over ice cream.

Serve in	Parfait glass
Rim	Unsweetened cocoa powder, shaved chocolate
Garnish	Whipped cream, maraschino cherry, shaved chocolate

Cheeky Girl

Full of bounce and vigor, the cheeky girl has no regrets and says what she wants. Serve this version with your highest heels and mini-est skirt, tuck a hibiscus blossom behind your ear, and gather the girls for a fun tropical night in.

SERVES 1

1 ounce coffee liqueur
1 ounce banana liqueur
1/2 ounce brandy
1/2 ounce coconut rum
1/2 medium banana, peeled
2 ounces cream (half-and-half or heavy cream)
1 cup ice

In a blender combine all the ingredients and blend until smooth. Serve in a large glass with a straw or a spoon.

Serve in	Parfait glass
Rim	Unsweetened cocoa powder, sugar of choice (granulated, colored, etc.), instant coffee powder, sweetened coconut flakes
Garnish	Paper umbrellas, chocolate shavings, sprinkles, remaining banana slices

Try adding in a cherry liqueur or a splash of grenadine for a fruitier flavor. For best results use a bright yellow, ripe banana with firm fruit.

Raspberry Cheesecake

Sensual and seductive, cheesecakes are a favorite treat for many. Serve this one to a crowd and revel in the smiles you receive! This recipe can be altered for different tastes, so have other liqueurs and syrup flavors on hand.

SERVES 1

1 tablespoon cream cheese, softened
1 ounce white crème de cacao
1 ounce black raspberry liqueur
2 scoops vanilla ice cream
1/2 cup crushed ice

In a blender combine all the ingredients and blend until smooth. Pour into a glass and serve.

Try cherry brandy for a Cherry Cheesecake, orange liqueur for an Orange Cheesecake, chocolate liqueur for a Chocolate Cheesecake, and crème de cassis for a Black Currant Cheesecake.

Serve in	Parfait glass
Rim	Graham cracker crumbs
Garnish	Graham cracker crumbs, grated chocolate, fresh whole raspberries

Between the Sheets

This very popular and well-known recipe varies in the amounts given for each ingredient, but the ingredients themselves stay the same. This recipe serves two, so turn down the bedspread and light the candles before serving!

SERVES 2

4 ounces brandy
3 ounces light rum
1 ounce triple sec
1 ounce freshly squeezed lemon juice

Shake all the ingredients in a cocktail shaker half-filled with ice until well chilled. Strain into glasses and serve.

For a sweeter drink, add a small amount of sugar syrup (page 42); for a less tart drink, use 1 tablespoon lemon juice. Some recipes give equal ratios for all ingredients, varying from 1/2 ounce to 1 ounce each.

Serve in	Chilled martini glasses
Rim	None
Garnish	Lemon slices

Mango Martini

A mango, eaten fresh, tastes refreshing and naughty at the same time. It may be the unsophisticated nectar that runs down your hand and over your chin, but with this elegant martini, you won't have to worry about any juicy messes.

SERVES 1

1 ounce mango rum
1 ounce light rum
1/2 ounce triple sec
1/2 ounce lime juice
1/2 ounce cranberry juice
1 ounce mango purée

Shake all the ingredients in a cocktail shaker half-filled with ice until well chilled. Strain into a glass and serve.

Serve in	Chilled martini glass
Rim	Sugar of choice (granulated, colored, etc.)
Garnish	Paper umbrella, cubed and skewered mango chunks, lime slices

> **Different flavors of cranberry juices, such as black cherry or raspberry offer a nice change of pace.**

Smartini Tip
Omit the rums and triple sec and substitute 1/2 teaspoon rum extract, freshly squeezed orange juice, and an increased amount of mango purée.

Twilight Coffees

There's no swaying a java junkie from their cherished beverage: coffee. An after-dinner version is an exquisite and traditional way to finish a meal. For a very late-night cup o' joe, you may wish to make decaf, but otherwise brew a quality, dark roasted bean, freshly ground. Instant coffee just doesn't cut it.

Hawaiian Coffee

Grapefruit juice, pineapple juice, brown sugar—bring the tropical flavor of the Hawaiian Islands to your coffee bar with this creamy concoction.

SERVES 1

3 to 4 ounces strong-brewed coffee, cold
1 1/2 ounces grapefruit juice
1 1/2 ounces pineapple juice
2 teaspoons brown sugar
1 scoop vanilla ice cream
Whipped cream

1. In a blender combine the coffee, juices, brown sugar, and ice cream and blend until creamy.

2. Pour into a glass and top with whipped cream to serve.

Serve in   Irish coffee glass

Rim   None

Garnish   Sprig of mint leaves, chocolate sprinkles

Add coconut rum, or some rum and coconut extracts, to enhance the tropical taste.

Espresso Martini

Since this intense martini uses real, brewed espresso it might not be the ideal cocktail for midnight sippers. Hardcore coffee lovers will adore the kick and may even ask for more!

SERVES 1

1 1/2 ounces vodka
1 ounce brewed espresso, cold
1/2 ounce coffee liqueur
1 teaspoon sugar syrup (page 42)

Shake all the ingredients in a cocktail shaker half-filled with ice until well chilled. Strain into a chilled glass and serve.

For a flavor variation, reduce the vodka and increase the coffee liqueur, or try a flavored vodka such as vanilla, chocolate, or coffee.

Serve in	Chilled martini glass
Rim	Instant coffee powder
Garnish	Sprig of mint leaves, chocolate sprinkles

Frozen Cappuccino

This frosty drink requires no brewing of coffee and is ideal for those hot and humid days when the thought of boiling anything makes your head swim. Mix in a splash of cinnamon liqueur if you wish to spice things up a bit.

SERVES 1

1/2 ounce Irish cream liqueur
1/2 ounce coffee liqueur
1/2 ounce hazelnut liqueur
1 scoop vanilla ice cream
1 teaspoon cream
1/2 cup crushed ice

In a blender combine all the ingredients and blend until smooth. Pour into a glass and serve with a spoon or a long straw.

A Cappuccino Cocktail can be made by mixing 3/4 ounce coffee brandy, 3/4 ounce vodka, and 3/4 ounce half-and-half with 1/4 teaspoon ground cinnamon.

Serve in	Irish coffee glass or parfait glass
Rim	Cinnamon sugar
Garnish	Ground cinnamon, cinnamon stick

Creamy Orange Buzz

This drink provides a welcome blast of espresso with a hit of creamy orange zing! Enjoy it as close to the end of dinner as possible, or use it as a pick-me-up before a long night of card playing with the gang.

SERVES 1

2 ounces brewed espresso, cold
2 ounces orange liqueur
1 1/2 ounces Irish cream liqueur

Add all the ingredients to a glass filled halfway with ice; stir and serve.

Serve in   Martini glass, brandy snifter, or old fashioned glass

Rim   None

Garnish   Orange twists

Use two orange twists to garnish, making sure to twist them over the drink itself to capture the flavorful citrus oils.

Irish Coffee

Rich, sweet, and yummy—is there any wonder why the classic Irish Coffee is the most widely consumed liqueur-and-coffee drink in the world?

SERVES 1

1 1/2 ounces Irish cream liqueur
6 ounces hot strong-brewed coffee
1 teaspoon sugar (preferably brown)
Whipped cream

Combine the Irish cream liqueur, coffee, and sugar in a mug and stir. Top generously with whipped cream and serve.

Serve in   Irish coffee glass or other mug
Rim   None
Garnish   Sprig of mint leaves, chocolate sprinkles

For a creamier version, stir in a little milk or cream before adding the whipped cream. You may also omit the sugar if you wish.

Café Brûlot

A long-time fave to serve in New Orleans and a traditional holiday drink, the creation of this dessert coffee can be complicated and dramatic. Here's an easy version that's simpler but just as delicious and popular!

SERVES 1

1 lemon twist
1 orange twist
1 whole clove
1 pinch ground cinnamon
1 teaspoon confectioners' sugar
8 ounces hot brewed coffee
1 to 2 teaspoons triple sec
1 to 1 1/2 ounces Cognac

1. Add the citrus twists, clove, cinnamon, and sugar to a mug.

2. Pour the hot coffee into the mug and add the triple sec and Cognac.

3. Stir until the sugar is dissolved, then remove the twists and clove, if desired. Serve immediately.

Sweeten with any type of sugar to taste. You can even use honey.

Serve in	Irish coffee glass or other mug
Rim	None
Garnish	Orange zest

Iced Coffee Frappé

This drink requires making coffee liqueur ice cubes ahead of time. The advantage is that you can store them in your freezer, so that when guests drop by you have them at the ready. The creamy, frosty flavor is worth the effort!

SERVES 1

Coffee liqueur ice cubes:
10 ounces strong-brewed coffee, cold
4 ounces coffee liqueur

Frappé:
5 coffee liqueur ice cubes
1 ounce vanilla vodka
2 ounces cream

1. To make the coffee liqueur ice cubes, mix the brewed coffee and the coffee liqueur in a medium bowl and pour into an ice cube tray. Each cube should contain about 1 ounce of the coffee mixture. Freeze at least two hours or overnight, until solid.

2. Prepare the frappé by blending the coffee liqueur ice cubes, vodka, and cream in a blender for 10 to 15 seconds, until the mixture is slushy. Pour into a glass and serve immediately.

Serve in	Irish coffee glasses or parfait glasses
Rim	Unsweetened cocoa powder
Garnish	Unsweetened cocoa powder, chocolate stir stick, vanilla bean pod

Once frozen, pop out the flavored ice cubes and store in a resealable plastic bag in the freezer. Then make more coffee liqueur ice cubes or regular ice cubes with the tray as needed.

Flavored Coffee

Another plain cup o' joe never needs to be a part of your after-dinner groove again. For the United Nations tour of marvelous varieties below, mix each of the ingredient combinations with 1/2 cup (4 ounces) hot, strong-brewed coffee in an Irish coffee glass or other mug. Serve hot.

EACH SERVES 1

Velvet Coffee
1 ounce crème de cacao (dark or light)
1 ounce triple sec
1 teaspoon brown sugar

Raspberry Coffee
1 ounce raspberry liqueur

Monk's Coffee
1 1/2 ounces hazelnut liqueur
1/2 ounce dark crème de cacao

Coffee Royale
2 ounces brandy

Café Almond
2 tablespoons almond liqueur

Café Isreal
2 tablespoons chocolate syrup
2 tablespoons orange liqueur

Café Columbian
2 tablespoons coffee liqueur
1 tablespoon chocolate syrup

Italian Coffee
2 ounces almond liqueur

Jamaican Coffee
1 ounce coffee brandy
3/4 ounce light rum

Mexican Coffee
1 ounce coffee liqueur
1/2 ounce tequila

Bavarian Coffee
1/2 ounce peppermint schnapps
1/2 ounce coffee liqueur

To mix things up a bit, try adding coconut rum or rum extract.

Index

Drinks with
Smartini variation